LIGH...
BOLT
BOOKS™

# Let's Look at
# Sloths

## Janet Piehl

Lerner Publications
Minneapolis

Lerner Publications Company
A division of Lerner Publishing Group, Inc.
241 First Avenue North
Minneapolis, MN 55401 USA

For reading levels and more information, look up this title at www.lernerbooks.com.

Library of Congress Cataloging-in-Publication Data

Piehl, Janet.
    Let's look at sloths / by Janet Piehl.
        p.    cm. — (Lightning bolt books™ — Animal close-ups)
    Includes index.
    ISBN 978-0-8225-7900-7 (lib. bdg. : alk. paper)
    ISBN 978-0-7613-6282-1 (eb pdf)
    1. Sloths—Juvenile literature.  I. Title.
    QL737.E2P54  2011
    599.313—dc22                               2009038533

Manufactured in the United States of America
4-44302-8718-6/1/2017

# Contents

# Hanging Sloths

## What do you see hanging in this tree?

It's not easy to spot. It's a sloth!

5

A sloth is hard
to see when it is
hanging in a tree.
Its fur looks a lot
like the tree branch
where it hangs.

A sloth has shaggy brown or gray fur. But tiny plants called algae often grow in a sloth's fur. Sloths move very slowly. So the algae grows quite well!

This sloth moves so slowly that algae grows on its fur.

The algae can make the sloth's fur look green. The fur blends in with the leaves in the rain forest.

The green algae on this sloth is the same color as the leaves.

**How does a sloth hang in a tree?**

It hangs upside down by its long claws.

The claws are like hooks. They help the sloth grip the branches. A sloth's claws grow on the ends of its toes.

All sloths have three toes on their back feet. Some kinds of sloths have three toes on their front feet. They are called three-toed sloths.

Three-toed sloths are the only sloths with a tail.

Other kinds of sloths have two toes on their front feet. They are called two-toed sloths.

# Sleeping and Eating

What do sloths do while they hang in trees? Almost everything! Sloths sleep in trees. They sleep most of the time.

# Sloths also eat in trees. They eat leaves, fruit, bark, and twigs.

This sloth munches on a leaf.

This sloth is grabbing a leaf with its claw.

Sloths use their long arms and claws to grab food from branches.

15

Sometimes sloths swing slowly from branch to branch to find food.

They may also eat the algae from their fur.

# Baby Sloths

Mother sloths even have their babies in trees. When a baby sloth is born, it clings tightly to its mother.

A baby sloth drinks milk from its mother at first. This is called nursing. A few months later, the baby sloth grabs and eats leaves and fruit on its own.

Soon it is ready to leave its mother. It finds a new place to hang in a nearby tree.

# Out and About

Does a sloth ever leave its tree? Yes! A sloth slowly climbs down about once a week.

It moves to another tree to search for food.

A sloth scoots along the ground on all fours.

# Sloths can't walk on two feet.

So many sloths move to different trees by pulling themselves forward with their claws. Other sloths crawl.

A three-toed sloth uses its front claws to move forward.

Sloths move slowly on the ground. But they move faster in the water.

Sloths can swim well.

# Sloth Predators

Leaving the trees can be dangerous.  It is easy for enemies to see sloths when they are not hidden in trees.

Predators may attack sloths. Predators hunt and kill other animals for food.

The sloth's predators include cats such as jaguars and ocelots.

An ocelot may hunt a sloth for food.

Snakes and harpy eagles also attack sloths. The sloth fights back with its long claws. It hisses and bites.

Harpy eagles attack sloths.

This sloth is safe. It slowly climbs a tree. It hangs. It sleeps. It wakes up to eat. Can you see the sloth?

# Sloth Range Map

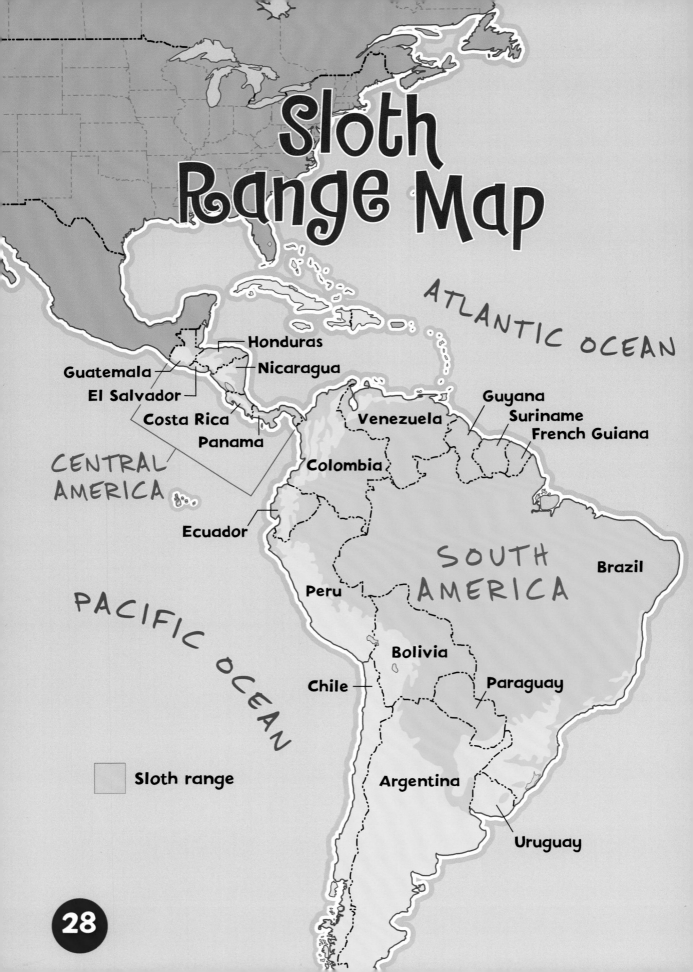

ATLANTIC OCEAN

Honduras

Nicaragua

Guatemala

El Salvador

Costa Rica

Panama

CENTRAL AMERICA

Ecuador

Venezuela

Guyana

Suriname

French Guiana

Colombia

SOUTH AMERICA

Brazil

Peru

Bolivia

Chile

Paraguay

PACIFIC OCEAN

Argentina

Uruguay

☐ Sloth range

# Sloth Diagram

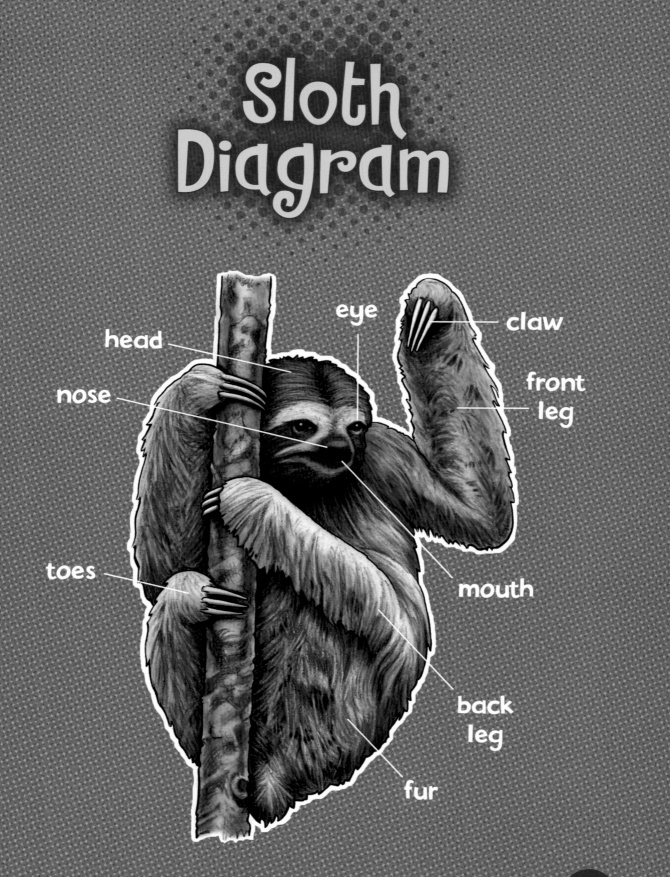

head

nose

toes

eye

claw

front leg

mouth

back leg

fur

# Glossary

**algae:** tiny plants that have no leaves, stems, or roots. The plants live in the fur of many sloths.

**nursing:** drinking milk from a mother's body

**ocelot:** a kind of wild cat. Ocelots sometimes attack sloths.

**predator:** an animal that hunts and kills other animals for food

**rain forest:** a dense woodland where it rains often. It is home to rich plant and animal life.